POLAND
and other
poems

POLAND
and other poems

by Lily Brett

*Drawings
by David Rankin*

SCRIBE

First published in Australia in 1987

Scribe Publications Pty Ltd
50 Weston St., Brunswick 3056

© Lily Brett and David Rankin, 1987

Typeset in Schneidler by Bookset Pty Ltd
Printed in Australia by Globe Press Pty Ltd

National Library of Australia
Cataloguing-in-Publication data:

Brett, Lily, 1946- .
   Poland and other poems.

   ISBN 0 908011 13 X.

   I. Rankin, David, 1946- . II. Title.

A821'.3

Photographs of Lily Brett and David Rankin
by Jacqueline Mitelman

For David

Contents

KADDISH FOR MY MOTHER

Acknowledgements

The poems, The Immigration Man,
An Ordinary City, The Intercontinental, Outside,
Where Were You, Your Sunwashed Skin, Everyone
Looks Depressed, Twenty-Three Zakatna Street, You
Arrived Back, After The War, Angry, I Look, To Me
and A Child made up the suite of poems called
Poland, which won the 1986 Mattara Poetry Prize.
They were published in the anthology, *An Inflection of
Silence*, ed. Christopher Polinitz (University of
Newcastle).

I would like to thank the editors of *Overland*. Several
of these poems first appeared in *Overland*.

The holocaust, the quality of our recognition of it as much as the fact, changed and continues to change, our world. And our other world, language. It is a distinction of Lily Brett's poetry that out of the silence after the bushfire, when ideas about the relations between culture and humanity burnt to the ground, a new language has grown. Painfully. On that skeletal tree, scorched almost to ash, minimal shoots appear. So stripped, so slight, we see them sharply: how tender they are, how freshly green. Language, altered forever, begins again.

Barrett Reid
16 August 1987

POLAND

Part One

The Immigration Man

I look at my feet
and feel myself spin
when the immigration man

taps his blue biro
violently
asking me
my nationality

Australian I say
he's holding
my passport
and why should he ask

he taps faster
and I feel
I might faint

could he be
one of the
Poles
who pointed you out

mother
who called back the Nazis
to say
you've missed one in this house
take her she's Jewish.

An Ordinary City

It looked like
an ordinary
city

long rows of
newly-built
Victorian facades

an
attempt
at graceful boulevards

gold-leafed
churches
standing proud

no
hostile
crowds

no
policemen
pointing pistols

no
locals
looking

for
bounty
on

Jewish
men women
and children

I wonder
whether
the man

sitting
in
the Krokodile Kafe

pointed
you
out to the Nazis

or
maybe
the lady

in
the
bread queue

knew
you
were Jewish

and
beckoned back
the Gestapo

it looked like
an ordinary
city.

The Intercontinental

Even in the intercontinental
at 120 American dollars a day
the toilet paper
bled purple lumps
and knots of brown bark

the square sachet
of bile-coloured
shampoo
resembled disinfectant
and was stolen

while we breakfasted
on 5 grams of coffee
50 grams of yellow cheese and 50 grams
of brittle black bread
in the elegant architecture of the morning room

a monochromatic huddle of waiters
stood silently ready to serve
and note your choice
instead of cheese you could choose
50 grams of cold meat or a 50 gram egg

and anything you left
was stealthily swept
from this grandly set table.

Outside

Outside silent lines
queue for soap shoes toothpaste
toilet paper or washing powder

zlotys can't buy these
luxury items
dollars are required
with dollars you might also find
paper pens pantyhose and proper clothes

a uniform grey
coats people's thoughts and faces
children wear plastic parkas
and absent expressions

the newly-rich
are flower growers
three freesias for half a week's work
but people
need to be cheered

market gardeners
are growing money
their hot houses
sit in the snow
sprouting carrots beetroots and beans

and alcohol
is easily available
a sweet
deep cerise vodka
is downed at every occasion.

Where Were You

Where in Warsaw
were you
when the ghetto was burning

that small city
of streets
crowded with corpses

and skinny remains
of uncles aunts
cousins and brothers
mothers and fathers

that they set alight
to burn
for days and nights

were you
watching in the middle
of that heated cheering crowd
on the Aryan side

while Fela
holding her baby
leapt from the top
of a blazing building

like a sparkler
spinning
through the sky

or did you cry
in excitement
as Moniek and his mother
exploded into the night

maybe you
were dazzled
by the display

when Pola
and then Adek
blasted
into the dark

and Shimon who was two
left
like a catherine wheel
somersaulting off the earth

were you
part of that flushed crowd
that clapped

here goes
another one
with her son

where in Warsaw
were you
when the ghetto was burning.

Mrs Potoki-Okolska

When I say
I want
to visit
Auschwitz

our Polish guide
an indefatigable
speedy
woman

like
you
mother

says
yes
of
course

she
lost
plenty

of
family
there
too

it
wasn't
just
Jews

like
you
mother.

Everyone Looks Depressed

Everyone looks depressed
deprived and distressed
and I feel cheerful

buoyed by their hardship
though I feel
ashamed
to think this
I am pleased

you've got
what you deserve
I whisper
to a man in the tram

who looks
the same age
as you
mother.

A View

When I feel
I will scream
if I see

one
more monument
to a famous general

the manic
Mrs Potoki-Okolska
acknowledges

that
this
is an emotional trip

she says
that when
I've seen

the
Jewish
bits

I
could
return

for
a
view

of
Poland.

On the Way to Lodz

On the way to Lodz
our tireless guide
insists we stop

at
Zelzowa Wola
Chopin's home

we see
Chopin's piano
Chopin's mother's piano

Chopin's bedroom
Chopin's mother's bedroom
Chopin's bathroom and Chopin's garden

I glare at the guide
who takes us past
Chopin's desk and Chopin's table

Mrs Potoki-Okolska
I stutter
are we going to Lodz

and again I feel
Lodz
doesn't exist

and
maybe
mother

I
will
never

touch
your
past

eventually
Mrs
Potoki-Okolska

leaves
Chopin
reluctantly

humming
La
Polonaise.

Part Two

This Grim City

They
call
Lodz

the
Manchester
of Poland

this
grim industrial
city

built
on
the textile industry

makes
Manchester

look
like
Monte Carlo.

In the Grand Hotel

In the Grand Hotel in Lodz
which certainly has seen
grander days

we sit
in a dining room
as big
as a football field

the tables are set
with silver
white starch
and gleaming glass

the menu
the length
of a novella

features
duckling
wild boar
roast deer
and herring

however
everything's off
except for pheasant

the pheasant
served
by four fussing waiters
on an enormous platter

has legs
that could shatter
you

this pheasant
possessed
12 inch pins

I ask
if they're sure
it is pheasant

and
cause
such a fuss

eating
this sinewy
outsize
drumstick

I
recover
fifteen shotgun pellets

the waiters rejoice
this validates
their claim of game.

On My First Morning

On my first morning
in the Grand Hotel
I leave the twin beds
linked with an iron bolt

leave the cushioned warmth
of the smooth eiderdown
of feather bolster
the linen bedding

I walk through the huge
bathroom and you
look at me
in the mirror

large lids creased
with sleep
a crazy mangle of hair
jutting up in the air

the same thin lips
the same high cheeks
the same forlorn
early-morning expression

and I have travelled
with my fear
and my suspicion
and my anger

and I am here
on the other side
of that dark moon
with you

mother.

People With Pallid Faces

People with pallid faces
limp hair
and lank expressions

stare
at
us

they
turn
in the streets

nudge
each other
in bus queues

point
in the foyer
of the five star hotel

I feel
like a recent arrival
from Mars

though
I'm wearing
cautious conservative clothes

and
have removed
my jewellery

maybe
it's my
clean hair

and
clear
complexion.

A Lunch

At lunch
with two barristers
and two surgeons

whose
positions of influence
I have decided

can
do me
no harm

the
indecipherable
blasts of barked Polish

frighten
me

at lunch
with a mouthful
of trout

half
chewed
I suddenly knew

all four
were the same age
as you

my
sweet-faced father

bilious
I rush
for the toilet

which
sits
ten feet

from
the
table

in
a
sweat

I hold
the broken
door

closed
with my
foot

and
cough
loudly

to
cover

my
own

violent
eruptions.

Zakatna Street

It is mid-day
a meek and sickly sun
casts a green tinge
over Zakatna street

the corner block
four graciously proportioned
concrete and brick floors
built by your father father

is intact
this city had
too many German inhabitants
to be attacked with bombs

nearby in Poludniowa street
are more of your father's apartments
and a palace
you once lived in

a thin shrivelled woman
on the fifth floor
says the caretaker downstairs
has lived there since nineteen-fifteen

the caretaker
Jengelef Boleswaf
who is eighty-three
tells me he remembers you well

I enter his
twelve feet by ten feet apartment
through a thick curtain of blankets
behind the front door

we speak
at a spotless table
while his dying wife
lies scrubbed and still

Jengelef nods his head constantly
he remembers you father
remembers you returning wounded
from the Polish army

he remembers your father
and says he had
a terrible temper
and you were afraid

of this fierce moustached man
who knew he was doomed
when he moved
to the ghetto

Jengelef is talking about my grandfather
father I am stiff
I don't want to miss
one syllable of this

I feel sick
and realise
I have forgotten
to breathe

Jengelef tells me father
that at twenty-three
you were quite a man
with a spirit for life

I tell him
you still have it.

Twenty Three Zakatna Street

A cloud-lit nipple of light
surrounds the moon
on Zakatna street

the street as deserted
as it must have been
when they emptied you into the ghetto

inside number twenty-three
I touch the tiled wall
of the hall with my cheek

walk up and down
the pale marble stairs
where father you ran
from boyhood to a strong young man

at eighteen
you had ice-cream
delivered by droshke

and wooed
dark-haired dark-eyed girls
in your open-topped Opel

inside the apartment
everything is as it was
the white-tiled heater climbs
from the floor to the ceiling

the round yellow-timbered couch
and chairs have hardly aged
the brown curved bed
carries the patch you carved

only the rich
could afford the internal toilet
whose pipes froze every winter
giving you nightmares

if they could put your family back
three brothers one sister
your mother and father
nothing would have changed

a cloud-lit nipple of light
surrounds the moon
on Zakatna street

the street as deserted
as it must have been
when they emptied you into the ghetto.

Part Three

At Eight O'clock

At eight o'clock
I walk along
Kilinskiego street

the still
black air
hardly moves

the moon
is in
mourning

I pretend
I am
a dragon

and breathe
warm swirls of smoke
into the cold

occasionally
an armed policeman
passes by

otherwise
there is
no sign of life

as
though
Lodz

has swallowed
its people
for the night

there is no noise
all doors
are shut

shop fronts
are
boarded up

I
hug
myself

and
remember
the smell

of
another
Saturday night

the
Boulevard
St. Michel

heady
with
perfumed expectation

and
polished lovers
and prouder couples

transient travellers
and
intertwined friends

or
Melbourne
meeting at fifteen

under
the clocks
at the station
in
my one-shouldered
Polynesian print

exuding
shrill
sophistication

another
policeman
marches past me

on
Kilinskiego
street

and
I
freeze

I
cannot
breathe

I
have
you here

mother

we
are
fifteen.

Your Sunwashed Skin

Your sunwashed skin
shines
in creamy silk

you sing
in
your square glass house

and
feed birds
figs

I came to Lodz
to see
if you lived

before
me
mother

in the centre
squat grey buildings
sit

on
either side
of black tram tracks

squashed snow
edges
dark doorways

blank windows are
shrouded
in rags and blankets

aged
paper
covers cracked panes

of
glass
in your old apartment

the
courtyard
you skipped in

on
Pomorska street
is small and bleak

the
Jewish school
72 steps

up
from
you

is
bolted
and barred

its
records
burnt

I came to Lodz
to see
if you lived

before
me
mother.

Pomorska Street

I have walked
through your days
mother

I have talked
with your
thoughts

I have breathed
the harsh air
mother

on
Pomorska
street

I have sat
on the black
steps

of your
cold
courtyard

and
wept

with
you
mother.

I Looked For You

I looked
for you
mother

on Pomorska street
on Pilsudskiego
street

in the school
on Poludnowia
street

I looked
for your mother
mother

in the ghetto
on Palacowa
street

I mothered
myself
mother

clutching
my crumpled leather bag
to my chest

and I will
mother you
mother.

If

If
with
my white biro

I could string
some strong words
into a thread

I would spin
myself a cocoon
a second womb

and
gently
tuck us in together.

At Seventeen

At seventeen
not
having seen

much
of
life

mother

you
were sent
into the ghetto

where
you saw
everything.

You Emerged

You
emerged

with

a
sharp voice

a
busy body

a
cold touch

a
distance

I
couldn't
cover

mother.

I Am

I
am

a
child

of
sunshine

and
light

and
bayside beaches

aren't
I

mother.

I Look

In cafes
I look
at the same face

on
separate
people

and
feel
myself

hypnotised

watching
mothers
with their mothers

and
daughters
with their daughters

and
mothers with mothers
and sons
and daughters

and
mothers with mothers
and their mothers.

To Me

To
me

you'd
always
been

honey
coloured

covered
with

a
glossy
sheen

of
sunshine

and
a
silk
shirt

although
I
knew

you
had

a
dark
past

when
I
walked

through
the
courtyard

black
and
bleak

in
Pomorska
street

I
could

place
you.

Falling

For days I have been
falling out of
myself

I sit in cafes
gripping
my shoulders

to stop
myself
dropping

I
feel
unplugged

pulled
from my
socket.

Angry

I
am
angry

I
dizzy
myself

fly
from
my skin

float
in
fright.

You Arrived Back

Your bones bumped into each other
your feet could hardly hold you

the rage that sustained you
for five years
slipped out of your grip

you contemplated death
but felt
too tired

when you touched clean sheets
you wept
for the first time

you ate everything they offered you
and brought it up
over and over again

and this is how you arrived back
in Pomorska street

and this is how
you conceived me.

A Child

I
feel
like

a
child

of
ash

a
child

of
screams

and
cries

a
child

of
promise

a
new
child.

Part Four

After The War

After the war
it made your ears ache
your skin creep
your head swim

to see
your possessions
belonging to them

to sit
with Mrs Polski
who used to be
the caretaker

while her gangly callow son
wallowed
in your father's suit

she served you cake
on china plates
that were part of your mother's dowry

and the grand piano
standing polished and proud
was your brother's most prized possession

and you could see
mother
that Mrs Polski
was surprised
to find you still alive.

You Could Look at Me

You could look at me
in my straight
black suit
and smooth stockings

you could look at me
wearing my Waltham
art deco watch
and my Tiffany ring

you could look at me
my mascara'd eyes
outlined and defined
my expression serene

serenity is my speciality
I exude calm
the way others
express excitement

you could look at me
you could look at me

you could look at me.

The Mother Tongue

The mother tongue
my mother
spoke with me

in
Feldafing
the D.P. camp

was
not
hers

it
was
German

imagine
endearments
echoing a Nazi staccato

then
we crossed the world
and switched to English

a
stumbling awkward
communication

which
I
picked up quickly

my
mother's poetic
Polish

seemed
incomprehensible
to me

and
was ditched
except for privacies

between
her
and my father

this
batch
of languages

hatched
a lack of subtlety
a severity

everything
was shouted
or stated

in
an uncomfortable
expression.

Today I

I know him
as the
panic phantom

cold air floats
from the folds
of his long black coat

he shakes
his bony fingers
and speaks in a broken baritone

do you want
to see
what trouble
really means

I have been
asked
this question
before

this ghost
and I
are very close

I know
his quivering fingers
and leap-frogging fears

we have lain
together
and I have stroked
his frozen ears

no
I say
don't explain trouble
to me today.

Displaced

I was born
in a displaced person's camp
and have often felt displaced

although
I don't think
you could tell

when I put
my perfectly symmetrical face
in place

they say
I look like a madonna
or the Mona Lisa

I don't know
if madonnas despair
or gasp for air

in strange locations
in spaces that are
too big too small
too dark too tall

do madonnas
check their front door
four times before being assured
it is shut

and do they
after securing the handbrake and gear stick
rush back to the car believing
it will slip downhill

I wonder if madonnas
have to hide
when their children
climb tall slides in the park

or can madonnas
walk in the dark
without imagining
packs of attackers

I comfort myself
maybe the Mona Lisa
wasn't always at ease.

Today II

I thread myself
through you
and I am in Lodz
in the ghetto

Punt Road
becomes Palacowa Street
it blackens
and shrinks

crowded
weeping
buildings
swim towards me

the sky
has drawn
a sombre cloak
over itself

I am alert
I search
for the Gestapo

I hold
my bread roll
firmly in my pocket

I have spotted
potatoes and beans
and am carrying them home

concealed
in the lining
of my coat

bold wings
sprout from me
I am bathed in bravery

I reach the end
of Palacowa street
I want
to raise my hands

and
spin around
in a circle
of cartwheels

I feed
your mother
and your father

I feed
you
mother

and I feed
you
father.

Today III

The sun is laughing
a high
strident
yellow laugh

a long
sniggering beam
reaches out
and squeezes me

I am
bleached
and breathless
I sweat

in the garden
under
the same
saffron star

fat ginger plants
and tall tuber roses
exude
a sensuous scent

topaz
marigolds
flutter their lashes
with pleasure

I
sit
at a white
wrought-iron table

my
black-stockinged ankles
rest against
its ornate base

displaced
I dream myself
somewhere else

I paint
a soft grey sky
a kind light

streets
of market stalls
and eager bargainers

rows
of squat apartments
filled with family

every block
has
another cousin

clutches
of aunties
visit me

I am
related
to everybody.

Today IV

In my
evenly-lit
open-plan
pale brick house

emerald
relfections
from the swimming pool
ripple across the ceiling

a curved crimson urn
cradles a hill
of ruby and amber
mangoes

svelte
black
chocolate sticks
line a slim silver platter

smooth prunes
proud of their plump flesh
recline
in a cut-crystal skillet

I sit
on the puckered and studded sofa
disconsolate
and disconnected

suspended
I invent
my death
and weep for myself

I spin
a large web
of sympathy
to break my fall

poor Lily poor Lily

I cheer myself up
I note how bereft
those I've left behind
will be

poor Lily poor Lily.

I Am Populated

I am populated again
and have to
talk to myself

argue
my case
listen to the opposing view

this
happens to me
periodically

I was born
in a country
whose inhabitants

murdered
those
who inhabit me

I was moved
to
Australia

and have been
at odds
with myself

longing
for
a less harsh light

a
cooler
climate

looking
for
a life

which
I
suspect

died
in
Poland.

KADDISH
FOR MY
MOTHER

Part One

Two Women

We are two women
who sit across
a white and gold-topped table

we are two women
one in her middle age
the other still strong not old

we talk
awkwardly warm
with each other

the central heating
hums
cheerfully around us

violet pansies bloom
in a small
purple pot

I try to throw off
the jealous child
who keeps swimming back to me

I am not your beautiful girl
your sweet six year old
with sausage ringlets bouncing

I am not the baby
you were ashamed
to conceive

I am not the fat teenager
who envied
your silver bikinis

I am not the mute mother
draped in black
as you waltzed in aqua satin

we are two women
one in her middle age
the other still strong not old.

These Words

I want
these words
to sit

on the edge
of
our conversation

to
hover above
the sentences

to
hardly
be heard

I'm
feeling
better.

My Thirty-Fifth Year

We sit
with our matching sets
of unevenly balanced
breasts

the same
tapered fingertips
and elegantly-angled
wrists

we see
one another
under large languid
lids

El Greco Goya and Picasso
painted our eyes
over hundreds of years
mother

but
you and I
have no-one
behind us

we cradle a past
of parched bones
and bodies
dismembered and headless

this
is my thirty-fifth year
and you
are sixty

today
I have brought you
huge bunches
of loose lilac

I want to cover you
with flowers
yesterday's zinnias
sit plump and pink in your kitchen

this tenderness
is new
it came to me
through another mother

it came to me
almost
too late
mother.

Mario Lanza

Mario Lanza is singing
Because You're Mine
and you are whistling
with him

yellow
sunshine
is filling
this blue glass house

you begin
your ritual
cleansing
of this vast nest

your brown arms fly
over the endless windows
until they are
as clear as air

Chanel no. 5
drifts from you
and mingles
with the disinfectants

your blazing red sun-dress
ends just above
your Monici of Rome
backless sandals

these are early years
and I am
chubby and small
and sausage-curled

and you are
still hopeful
still eager
still child-like

and no-one
can
tell
mother

that
you were
once

left
in a pile
of corpses

a bedraggled remnant
a scrappy traveller
in Hitler's demonic hotel

The Photograph

Today I looked
at the photograph
I took
days after they diagnosed you

you are wearing
one of your
cream silk shirts
over a grey tailored skirt

lightly spotted stockings
with a lavender hue
and purple Yves St Laurent
high-heeled shoes

your sun-coloured skin
still gleams
and golden lights
shine from your carefully coiffured hair

your lipstick and mascara
are in place
but your face is thin and strained
and it is plain that you are dying

days ago
before that slow phone call
the surgeon awkwardly
warning me

things look nasty
he said
nasty
mother

nasty
the word whirled around the room
them jammed itself
against my chest

nasty
mother
it was your death
he was nervously skirting

days ago
I was running around you
with that old anger
snapping me like elastic bands

the jealous fat child
standing sausage-limbed
on St Kilda beach
next to your bikini'd smile

and I couldn't see
mother
I couldn't see.

Patting Yourself

Patting yourself
you said
that your normally flat
stomach was swollen

I spat out a glare
then coughed
and tried to wipe it
into a smile

the crooked hooked-nosed witch
who lives in me
was screaming
vanity vanity

she cackled memories
in my ear
of years watching you
tanned and taut

stepping elegantly
among the ti-trees
in your backless bathers
and strapless sandals

while I plodded along
lumpy-limbed
in the wrong
shirred and frilled swimsuit

I grimaced
and
dismissed the witch
for her disfigured vision

I said I was sorry
mother
and maybe
you were constipated

together
we drank lemon tea
with tiny cloves
floating through it

the next day tests
showed
that cancer
was bloating your belly

and
me and the witch
mother
we screamed and screamed.

I Thought

I thought I would change
mother

I thought kind words would
float from my mouth

and pirouette
in a pink tutu

I thought I would hold
you

breathe
your exotic scent

feel your hands
for the first time

I thought I would touch
you

and
be touched by you

smile
at your crooked English

mixed
with Polish and Yiddish

I thought I would listen
to you

I thought I would see
you

instead
the wicked witch

waved
her daily wand

and all my words
came out wrong

wild swipes
landed

where
they didn't belong

I thought I would change
mother

when
I knew

you
were dying.

Part Two

104

Looking After Me

You are dying
and
you say

on Friday
you will cook
a goulash

and
can the children
stay

and
I already
feel you've gone

feel
lost
abandoned
motherless.

The Elegant Scent

The elegant scent of Miss Dior
which hovered in thick wisps
around you
has gone

the white and black satin
beaded cocktail dress
rests with the aqua taffeta
tailored suit

your lace underwear
and silk stockings
are still there

silver bikinis that glittered
against your summer tan
lie quiet

jars of creams
and lotions
and scrubs

cluster with
rows of
perfumes

and
you
mother

lie
limp in
your bed

your
ragged
small head

hardly
dents
the fine feathered pillow.

Honey-Coloured

Your
beautiful
face

its honey-coloured
sultry
pout

a bit like
Gina
Lollobrigida

has
wasted
away

the
sides
have disappeared

the
eyes
are enlarged

the
nose
is nothing but bone

the
lips
grim

your
beautiful
face

its honey-coloured
sultry
pout

a bit like
Gina
Lollobrigida

has
become
a skull.

Last Week

Last
week
mother

I thought
you couldn't look
worse

today
the sides of your face
have fallen away

your stiff neck
leans
forward

burdened
with responsibility
for your head

your poor feet
shuffle
after one another

your bloated legs
can hardly hold
you up

you clasp a cup
with wrists
finer than china

your thin lips
have
disappeared

around
your
growing teeth

your
eyes
are like

two
craters
on a ragged moon

last
week
mother

I thought
you couldn't look
worse.

My Mother is Dying

My mother is dying
and she sits
with pink lipstick
and her Christmas tan

on
white lace-cornered
linen sheets

with
mascara'd eyes
and a sweet expression

and I sit
grim
and anxious

and
abandoned.

We Do Not Move

We do not move
in a cocoon
no ease envelops us

a chill
swills
around the room

my fingers
grip each other
my tongue is stuck

what is missing
mother
has always been absent.

The Limbs

The limbs
you wound around
yourself

in yoga positions
are
stiff

you breathe deeply
before
you speak

your pink jacket
suggests
a cosiness

you were so clean
mother
and now you leak

the bum my father slapped
a thousand times
is flat

your beautiful skin
is green
and creased

your red hair
has returned
to grey

two men
with a stretcher
take you away

you
smile

big-teethed and wide-eyed
a crooked fairy queen
going for a ride.

Your Beautiful Face

Your normal
voice
is hoarse

you mime instructions
with
desperate gestures

your thin fingers
stab
the air angrily

your belly
is
bloated

your beautiful face
mother
has caved away

leaving you
looking
crooked.

The Angry Witch

You are the angry witch
with your flat hair
sharp chin and thin lips

your yellow skin
hollows into ochre
around your eyes

slim whisps
of damp red curls
sit in your stringy neck

your cold mouth
continues
to chill me

you are the angry witch
of my picture
mother.

Your Shoulders

Your shoulders
like a wire
hanger
hold your frame

your back
and hips
have dropped away

your head
a dark yellow knot
on your neck

is this
what is left
mother

is this
what is left
of that iron grip.

An Angry Shade

Your face
is an angry shade
of ochre

dried white spittle
sticks
at the side of your lips

your beautiful hooded lids
are brown
and creased

your grim teeth
have
grown

your thin wrist
is still
flicking orders

and
I am
frozen

mother
in your
yellow spell.

Lilac Lace

You have dressed yourself
in lilac lace
with red ribbons

and lie
on white satin-edged
linen

your lips
are
painted pink

your
red hair
is combed and waved

it took
two
slow hours

to arrive
at
this fresh start

which
is
stained

by
the bile
that jumps from your mouth

and
leaves
large green spots

on
this small piece
of your picture

you cry
while
you wipe up.

My Picture

Your dark brown skin
has become
green

the whites of your eyes
have turned to
mud

your scalp
is a brilliant
yellow

your small
head
leans

giving you
a crooked
look

you fit
my
vicious

picture
mother.

To Fool the Fox

In
your
hospital bed

dressed
as a grandmother
to fool the fox

in
pink frills
and polished lips

you
call me
sweety

too
late
mother

I
have emptied
your tenderness

and
this grim vixen
slips through

dry-eyed
and
hard-hearted.

Air

Air
constantly erupts
from you

your stomach
is screaming
its own
slow concerto

your skin
is beaming
bright amber

your voice
floats like a ghost
from your mouth

the arrogant eye
that observed
my every gesture
has wandered

the
deathly glare
has gone

leaving
hot smelly
air.

A Dark Mouse

You lie
like
a dark mouse

yellow-eyed
and
small-faced

once
you
breathed fire

in
this
glass house

with
cocktail
gowns

and
silk
stockings

and
plunging
bras

with
plenty
of
uplift

now
the air
is flat

perfumed
with
suppositories

and
mother

you
are

my
little
mouse.

You Sleep

You sleep
with your eyes and mouth
wide open

as though you are frozen
in the middle
of a terrible scream.

The Slow Dream

Everything
in this slow dream
is tranquil

you call
me
Liebala

and
appear
peaceful.

Day and Night

You are bilious
day
and night

it is worse
than the pain
you explain

and
apologise
for the awful sight.

On Your Side

You lie on your side
black bile
slides from the corner of your mouth

I sit nearby
hugging
my crumpled leather handbag

clasping it to my chest
like a precious
child

every now and then
you moan
and creak

your fingers
and lips
twitch

your heart
misses
several beats

and I cling
to
my bag.

Part Three

I Have Never Known

Mother I have never known
where you ended

I have worn us blended
for forty years

I have walked through Melbourne
as though it were Warsaw

on guard for the Gestapo
in fear of informers

alert
to any menace in the air

and I have bought boxes
of eggs and potatoes and bread

and cheese and cherries
and pickled cucumber and herrings

to put aside
for leaner times

and I have had my nightmares too
of what I might not have been able to do

and I know how every event
a knock at the door a burst of rain

a child's complaint
a husband's breakfast

is always a question
of life and death

and I measure myself mother
against imagined obstacles

and am left
lacking.

A Look

I took a look at that photograph
the one that was left
under a pile of letters
on the kitchen bench

the one in which your long arms
are making an announcement
you look solid and strong
mother

not long after that
they said you had cancer
and I have other photographs
that show you cracked

battling to hang on to yourself
you are dressed in blue Louis Feraud
but the clothes emphasise what is lost
and float on your fleshless frame

I have been unable to face
your face
in the photograph
on the kitchen bench

unable to look at those large eyes
before they grew outsize
unable to see the vigorous hips
before they disappeared

now all of you has gone
and I have a box of photographs
and the same shaped shoulders
and the face we shared

and I have been scared
mother

scared to take a look at you
in case I catch the cancer too

oh I have been scared
mother.

The Village Belle

The supermarket
manager
saved you
weekly specials

the steely-eyed
mean-beaked parrot
in the pet shop
proffered you pieces of corn

Mr Gruner
the butcher
minced your beef
separately

and Mario
ceremoniously
brought his fruit
to you

the best pears
perfumed paw paws
and strawberries
from Queensland

you ignored
the miraculous display
of cakes
in window after window

mountains
of striped marzipan slices
poppyseed strudel
and chocolate macaroons

the cafes
leaking
their hypnotic aromas
never lured you

your strong brown legs
would fly past
until you reached
the beach

and
there
from a beaded Italian
rafia bag

you fed
a loud ragged assembly
of seagulls
bread.

Mrs Baberoshky

Mrs Baberoshky
approaches me
in the foyer
of Melbourne's grandest hotel

I am sitting in a corner
wishing I were on the floor
so I wouldn't feel
as though I was falling

hello darling
and what is wrong
she asks
I say I haven't been feeling well

since
the death
of my mother

I attempt to smile
through this dizziness
I look sick and stiff

Mrs B. thinks it is her business
to pep me up
to set me straight
to put me on the right path

listen darling
you've got to be strong
it is wrong to look so bad
and what about your dad

and
your children
and
your husband

as she departs
I hear her shout
it is shocking
it is shocking.

Poland

What do you want
to go to Poland for
you screamed

your golden face
frozen
and distorted

the Poles
were worse
than the Germans

small children
in the towns around
the camp

would kick us
when we walked to work
in our striped rags

grown men
would throw
a piece of bread

and
nearly die with laughter
while we fought each other

oh
those nice Poles
those good people

what do you want
to go to Poland for
you wept

they
won't let you leave
so easily

something
terrible
will happen

Liebala Liebala
please
why go

you know
after the war
there was a miracle

not
one Pole
did know

about
what happened
to us

you
could smell
the flesh

burning
for
kilometres

the sky
was red
day and night

and
the Poles
didn't notice

Liebala Liebala
please
don't go.

I was shouting

I was shouting at my son
the young medical student
the small boy
you adored

I was shouting about
coming home late
I was shouting about
appreciating

parents
when
you still
had them

parents
while
they were still
alive

my
lips
froze
in mid-verse

how
had
this old script

slipped
out
of my mouth

they
were
your lines
mother

I remember
the repetitious lyrics
the angry stanzas

no-one
has
better
parents

you
will cry
on our graves

but
it will be
too late

I remember
those
snappy
epics

at seventeen
you owned
your school uniform
and your Sabbath dress

you were not jealous
of my pink Pontiac
my French clothes
my expensive shoes

mother
you
envied me
my parents.

A Chignon

I was fourteen
and had been
practising
a chignon

my brown
out-of-control curls
pulled back
like Audrey Hepburn

I was pretending
that the bulky vision
in pink gingham
was not me

I was radiant
I was throwing
myself
an approving smile

when you
burst into the bathroom
like a hot volcano
spitting sharp lava

do you think
you are
a film star
you shouted

Sophia Loren
Lana Turner
maybe
Elizabeth Taylor

at your age
I gave
mathematics
tuitions

to pay
for a better school
Jews
could go to

hair hair
you howled
how can hair
help you

knowledge
education
can never be taken
from you

and
clutching
your head
you wept and wept

the next day
looking awkward
and crooked
you took me

across
the street
to Mr Brown
the barber

Mr Brown
snipped
and shaved
and clipped

and
clutching
my head
I wept and wept.

A Death

It was like a death
in the family
you said
a death a death

a death
in this
scrappy snapped
family

four
fragments
fastened together
by death by death

I was leaving
I said
tough
if it is a death

tough
mother
I was seventeen
and I left

a death a death
you whined
and I
blocked my ears

you made
and unmade
my bed
for years

years
later
I listen
to myself

I
who was never left
by a mother and father
three sisters and four brothers

I
who was never left
to die
can't say goodbye

see you
see you
I repeat
see you

a magic mantra
a good-luck charm
a guard against
a death a death.

At Night

At night
while we ate
goulash with rice
or schnitzels and vegetables

a baked veal brisket
smoked sausage and cabbage
roast chicken
or fried whiting fillets

you stood
near the sink
and pulled apart
a slab of bread

and
observing
a silent mysterious rite
you ate

sometimes
it was
fresh rye
pitted with caraway seed

or
sweet
plump plaited
challah

pitch black
pumpernickel
pale bagels
a raisin loaf

sometimes
you crunched
the corregated crust
of a milk-filled Vienna

sometimes
when you had
finished
your granular provisions

you would tell us
how in the ghetto
stale bread
was prized

for
it required
much more
chewing.

I Was Dancing

I was dancing
in my black skirt
and black stockings
nodding my head

making
slow movements
with my legs
swivelling my shoulders

throwing back
my straightened hair
to the jazz
in the air

now and then
I gazed
at the clarinet
player

as Aryan
as Aryan
as the Germans
would have ordered

I was dancing
in my black skirt
and black stockings
nodding my head

when
out of the night
you arrived

a golden streak
rubbed in
by an errant genie

her mother's here
her mother's here
the whispers
filled the smoky air

where are the lights
you shouted
screaming
against the music

what
do these girls
want to do
in the dark

it is ten o'clock
time to go
you will be better off
at home

at home
my father
took me aside

you have
to remember
your mother
didn't have

years of dancing
dates with
young men
boyfriends

she
married me
at sixteen

my family
was
still rich

your
mother's father
thought

that
she would be
better off

with
me
in the ghetto.

Winter

In winter
in our centrally
heated house
we sweltered

outsize pipes
pumped
hot air around
day and night

I woke
each morning
with swollen eyes
and fat fingers

and was
forbidden
to open
my bedroom window

it is cold
cold cold
cold can kill you
you told me

the winter
of 1942
was the coldest
you said

you slept
on the floor
in your clothes
and shoes

five of you
bunched together
like
harnessed bananas

the walls
inside
shimmered
with ice

your burned
the skirting boards
and drawers
for fuel

and
kept the floorboards
to keep out
the rats

your father
used
two table legs
the beds

his chairs
and the sides
of the stairs
for firewood

and your brother
dismantled
his window sills
for kindling

and people
died frozen
pleading
in the streets.

Tales

The ghetto tales
I most hated
were about potato peels

the extravagance
of potato peel patties
steamed in a skillet

the good luck
of potato peel soup
thickened with sawdust

potato peels
it was
too pathetic

and
felt worse
than the stories

of
children
dying in the streets

and
relatives killing each other
for a piece of bread

and
trainload after trainload
vanished.

The Excrement Cart

On the twenty-fifth
of every month
the excrement cart
came into your neighborhood

two men or women
pulled the wagon
from the front
and two pushed at the back

the smell thickened the air
for hours before
these out-house emptiers
reached Palacowa street

by the time
the rickety cylindrical vehicle
arrived
it was amost overflowing

its contents
lurched over the sides
at every
upraised cobblestone

leaving
an abstract ochre
clotted trail
along Palacowa street

there was no shortage
of volunteers
for the career
of "fekalist"

the position
carried
extra rations
of bread and soup

sometimes
families
worked
these wagons

the children
could hardly hold
the long-handled ladle
that was used as a scoop

the fekalists looked
more worn
more drawn
more sickly

and after a few months
they retired
with
tuberculer lungs

sometimes
one
of them
survived

one evening
in
Melbourne
you introduced me

to Regina Kindler
a small woman
with oddly effervescent
hair

while she was chatting
she dabbed perfume
from a small silver bottle
behind her ears

on the back
of her wrists
between her breasts
on her neck

she dabbed
and dabbed
with quick
flicking gestures

poor Regina
you said
to me
later

sometimes
one
of them
survived.

My Eleventh Birthday

Do you remember
mother

the morning
of my eleventh birthday

you were
at Arnaldo's

having your hair
tipped with golden lights

and I was home
alone

and I wondered
what potato peels

would
taste like

I cooked
some up

and
was half-way

through
my first mouthful

when
you returned

and
you mother

who had never
laid a hand

on
either of her daughters

shook
me

until
I fainted.

164

The Cake

On the fifth of December
before dawn

in the blackness
of Palacowa Street

your mother arrived
with a surprise

it was
your eighteenth birthday mother

you were living
a married life

with your husband
his mother and father and brother

in one room
in the ghetto

Rooshka Rooshka
she whispered loudly

in the
still curfewed air

I have baked you
a cake

my
darling daughter

I sold
my blue woollen dress

with the mink trim
the one I wore to your brother's barmitzvah

to Mrs Zimmerman
for thirty-six saccharin

and a kilo
of thick potato peels

from the kitchen
that peels with a knife not a peeler

I minced the clean peels
and added

two cups of chopped
turnip and beetroot tops

some baking soda
salt saccharin and washed coffee grounds

for
extra texture

the mixture
fitted beautifully

in
my baking dish

with
a bit of water

oh
Rooshka Rooshka

my
beloved daughter

I have baked you
a cake.

I Am Mixing

I am mixing minced beef
having added salt eggs pepper and bread
six fat capsicums wait
with their gaping mouths

for their filling
I feed them
spoonful by spoonful
engrossed

in this
spiritual
ritual
I am caught

I am caught
by the small scenes
and quick pictures
which swim violently towards me

I remember you
wide-eyed
trying to blink yourself back
to consciousness

it makes me cry
mother
to think of you blinking
like that

you were trying
to listen

trying
to stay alive

blinking
and blinking

as though
it were sleep

not
death

you
were fighting.

One Dream

There was one dream
that came
time and time again
and left

you pale
and breathless
and quiet
for days after the visit

this nocturnal serpent
rattled you back
to the ghetto
you were seventeen

and so thin
your plaits
were thicker
than your wrists

you worked
in the church
The Most Blessed
Virgin Mary Church

here
soft loot
taken from deported Jews
was stored

mountains
of eiderdowns
and hills of pillows
filled the church

lying
like limp bodies
mourning
their owners

leaning
on the tiled walls
and spilling into
the crypt

and
The Most Blessed
Virgin Mary
smiled benignly

while
the feathers
and down
were sorted

and
packaged
to be shipped
to Germany

in
your cold dream
mother
you fall

into those
poor
slumped
doonas

and
drown
in
the down.

The Sound of Cheering

The sound of cheering
crowds
shakes the ground
around your grave

the red scent
of tomato sauce and beer
hovers
in the air

Springvale
the name
is pink and green
and promises

dreams
it does
not
deliver

Carlton is playing Melbourne
Australian Rules
football
hooligans

you always called them
maniacs
they punch and bump
each other

Australian men
you told me
again and again
live in pubs

and
beat
their wives
for recreation

Jewish boys
they know
how to behave
to women

I visit you now
and listen
to the sirens
and the screams

oh mother
what strange company
you keep
on cold weekends

what a strange audience
to absorb
what a strange cabaret
to take part in

what strange neighbours
you are bedded beside
a long way
from Lodz

oh mother
what a strange place
you have lain in.

Oh Mother

I thought
mother

you would
bowl the cancer over

wrench it away
with your anger

shred
those scrambled cells

death
tried to talk to you before

mother

in
the ghetto

in
Auschwitz

after the war
you thought about killing yourself

when you found
you were

the only one
left

you
couldn't

you wouldn't give death
the pleasure

you moved
to this blue country

and patched yourself up

with a house a husband
and children

cocktail gowns perfumes
nail polish

a suntan dinner dances
glamorous entrances

while death danced its tango
around someone else

you fed birds
every morning

and cleaned
ceaselessly

oh
mother

I
thought

you would
bowl the cancer over.

Part Four

I Have Been Away

I have been away
riding a slow train
for two days
away in a strange country

I know the landscape well
each sharp ridge
each carpeted escarpment
the sweet hills carved from a forged dream

this is the land of the fat queasy moon
where stars cry their eyes out
and the sea growls and mutters
and the wind howls a pitiful arpeggio

and the screaming green witch
streaks across the town
singing a stinging lullaby
on her new broom

yesterday and the day before
I returned from my daily visit
with the aquamarine-eyed teacher
who keeps me in tune

and I was gone
five minutes after I had returned
I went sailing off
from my Alain Delon designed bed

I went sailing off
in a boat built with beautiful jewels
each one polished slowly under my pillow
over years

and assembled
in my careful fixed hand
a waterproof cocoon
you can squeeze and squeeze

and huff and puff mother
I won't leave this room
you can huff and puff
you won't blow my house down

I went sailing off
and on the way to the dazed kingdom
the sky shook an angry finger at me
and a curved bird let out a long hoot

where are you where are you it hooted
and swooped in a black circle around me
until my hair struck out in a wild gesture
and frightened the snarling fowl

I went sailing off
into your horror mother
and gave birth to your nightmare
and bled all over your screams

I went sailing off
into the mud into the barracks
mud mud mud on my blood
and my mouth brimming with barbed-wire teeth

and the only tree that was left
was slow and depressed
and the flies looked ragged and tired
and the poor huddled clouds wept and wept.